Āria

Āria

Jessica Hinerangi

AUCKLAND
UNIVERSITY
PRESS

First published 2023
Reprinted 2023
Auckland University Press
University of Auckland
Private Bag 92019
Auckland 1142
New Zealand
www.aucklanduniversitypress.co.nz

ISBN 978 1 86940 991 3

Published with the assistance of Creative New Zealand

A catalogue record for this book is available from the National Library of New Zealand

Design by Duncan Munro
Cover and internal artwork by Jessica Hinerangi, 2023

This book was printed on FSC® certified paper

Printed in Auckland by Ligare Ltd

*Dedicated to any displaced or whakamā
mokopuna trying to reconnect with who they are.
Your tūpuna are right beside you.*

Hā

Kia pupuri te manawa
o ōku tūpuna.
Kia whakamana i taku ārero,
mā te reo taketake i tukua mai ai e rātou.
Kia mau, kia ita,
ki ngā taonga tuku iho ā rātou mā.
Ahakoa ngā piki me ngā heke,
ka whakatutuki i tā ōku tūpuna
i wawata ake ai.
He kākano ahau i ruia mai i Rangiātea
ā, ka tipu tonu.
Tihei, mauri ora!

Breathe in, breathe out.
I shall carry the strength
of my ancestors before me.
And my tongue shall be strengthened by the ancient reo
I have inherited because of them.
I shall hold on tightly,
to the many sacred gifts passed down by them.
And despite the rises and falls of hardship,
I shall fulfil the dreams my ancestors have for me.
Because I am a seed that was planted in Rangiātea,
my growth is inevitable.
Tihei, mauri ora!

Contents

1. Pōtangotango

Dear Tūpuna 1

I am well. Eating lots of pasta and vegetables, going for walks in the ngahere, socialising with other artists, swimming in emerald lakes, visiting whānau.

I hope you're ok with the mahi I'm doing. I assume you'd let me know if you weren't. Every day I'm trying to pry open my superlunary skull to make way for your messages and magnetic vibrations. Like a dam bursting under pressure, or the tooth snapping away from my koro's jaw when he tried to eat a brandysnap at Christmas, my little human head cracks from the weight of your tohu and tāwara. I am afraid of us sometimes. I am especially afraid of the missionaries, the lawyers, the traitors to the cause. They seem to overshadow the nurses, the guides and the gardeners. I avoid talking to you, but I know if we're ever gonna get anywhere, I have to listen. There is violence in me. There is rage. There is shame. Witi Ihimaera once said to suck it out, like snake venom. Suck and spit, suck and spit. Can we heal together? Perhaps now you're an ancestor you feel differently about what went on out here?

Once, I confided in my mother about my panic attacks. How I had to walk out in the middle of every lecture. How I visited the emergency room most weeks because I thought I was dying. She told me it was intergenerational trauma triggering my fight or flight. I remember telling a friend this and they laughed at how non-clinical it sounded.

I am a hypochondriac and I am testing out different kai in the car beside the hospital every day; waiting for an allergic reaction I will never have. The ultimate test will be when I try kawakawa berries for the first time in Whatamango Bay – there is no hospital near there. What if my body rejects the fruit, and that is like Papatūānuku saying that I am not good at being Māori.

People say Māori love this and Māori eat these things and you can't be Māori and not love kina ... I don't like kina so how can I be Māori? I have the palate of a child and the nervous system of an old white woman. I watched shows like *House* and *Shortland Street* way too early so now I think I'm sick all the time. I grew up asking my parents every night before bed if I have any 'signs or symptoms'. When I finally had something wrong with me, the doctor said it was stress and I believed him because I do worry too much and I was trying not to be the annoying hypochondriac everyone expected me to be.

In the weeks before surgery I kept my pepeha on a piece of paper in my bra and waited for permission from you. I hoped we'd meet up while I was under. Instead, it was just dark and all I felt were tubes and a rib cage that grated against itself like dry sea shells. In recovery I watched too much TV. While infomercials played I noticed the tī kōuka out the window, and they were nodding their heads, nagging me to go outside. I miss warmer winds.

My matakite friend keeps asking if you've visited me yet. I wonder if there is something wrong because I haven't seen any glowing figures beside my bed as of late. I saw my great nanny once during a meditation. Then again, I guess she was just me. But you are me anyway, I am you, so it works. I am visited in my facial expressions, my thought patterns, my inner dialogue. I only just saw a photograph of my great-koro for the first time and he has my koro's ears. Ahakoa he iti, he pounamu. I treasure all the little things that connect me to you, e te tūpuna.

I have begun to write our names again. On papers and drawings, I've started introducing myself at parties and functions, cafes and classes, with the names that were left behind in time. They had to be left so that you could fit into the Pākehā world.

A name holds mana. We hold the name as we hold tā moko, as tā moko holds whakapapa, as whakapapa holds our babies, as our babies hold our breath, as breath holds mauri, as mauri holds what is true. Ahakoa he iti, he pounamu. When I was little I didn't really know our names, I thought we only had two. Now I know, I walk with them again, I walk in them again.

When Mum taught us we were Māori, I assumed we were Kāi Tahu because we were born in Ōtepoti. Before I learned the word colonisation, I just thought perhaps we were all from where we were born. I didn't know we were actually from Taranaki and Hokianga, and then beyond to Hawaiki. I didn't know about urbanisation. I didn't know we had been dislocated long before I formed a blur inside the tummy. I was ten when I clicked that we had left so long ago, and though you're on Māori land, you're not really home. Not until you look at the photographs and trace the maps with your stubby little fingers, and learn about Parihaka and the dog tax, the eruption of Mt Tarawera, and the Native Schools Act.

I dream of eels every few weeks. I've said it before, I'll keep saying it, because Whiteness makes Māoriness feel so thin and frail sometimes. I worry a lot. But I'm learning to let my whakapapa speak for itself. My Pākehā identity sits with my Māori and it's awkward. Sometimes one doesn't like to give room to the other. In order to get the dishes done and bring the firewood in, I have to disassociate. Balancing the Pākehā 'how can you help yourself?' with the Māori 'how can we help you?' is a study of how we bleed out into each other.

I've noticed that my bedroom mirror has three sides. I've ploughed my flesh and boiled my cells, ready to sew and serve, white high neck lace over a collar bone as restless as winter waves beyond a dark harbour, green and red port lights piercing the narrowing eye sockets, sunken blue prints. I glance starboard to the first face of my Māori grandfather, who peers back at me, uncertain, or very certain, I can never tell, to the second face of my Pākehā grandmother who is bookended between tarot cards and spiked trifle pudding. I have many faces, all of which star their way back to Rarohenga, where the ocean is red and the first karanga squeezed itself out of the taiawa of Papatūānuku with a vibrato that caused tectonic plates to shudder. My bedroom mirror has three sides. The two it took to make me, and the one that shimmers in between. I am learning every day how to receive your aroha.

With love,
your mokopuna.

Bones

Lolling back in the bath
like the tongue of a taniwha
slinking out of glassy āria,
belly out and purposeful,
a naked, hairy marakihau,
obsidian canines and incisors
trailing toward my centre fold,
you could almost see me
cut into pieces,
split like the wood of the
flagpole hacked down
– tap tap tap taonga –
– rich karukaru –
I am patient yet
desperate to know,
pleased to do the mahi,
but gasping for a break.
Through my studies I read
Keri Hulme writing
over and over
'where are your bones?'
I wonder where mine lie,
where they rest,
where they are hidden . . .
Where are our bones?
Why will you not share with me
my bones?

Where is my tongue?
On display, a trophy of war.
Where is my tikanga?
Kept in the basement.
Where is my mana?
Locked in the museum.
And where are my whānau?
Scattered like dandelion seeds,
from the grating city,
to the harnessed horizon.

Where will we go?
How can we move forward
If we do not look back?

Barbie girl

I draw moko kauae on my Barbies
and then I make them kiss.
I hide under my bed rehearsing
sexy scenes until I get caught.

'Don't do that stupid,
don't be disrespectful.
That's tapu stuff.'

I learn the word 'tapu' after
visiting the Tangata Whenua
exhibit at the museum as a kid.
See how dark and spooky it is?
See all the glass and the signs
that say 'don't touch'?
That's you. That's part of you.
Don't touch it.

Big white almonds big wooden hands,
an ill-lit room filled with a booming voice,
dust in my eyes and sand on the floor,
shells and stuffed birds,
skeletons and splinters,
for a kid this is scary,
and I want to go to the
toy store instead.
I want to play.

I hide in the harakeke looking for fairies,
mushroom circles, and kēhua,
I realise I like girls as well as boys
when I read a picture book about a
beautiful woman who is kidnapped by
a taniwha. I ship myself with all the protagonists
and hide my shame in Wattpad fanfiction.

I drive up the coast in my shiny convertible
wearing $2 shop tiki keychains as earrings,
Cali Cool Beach Girl from Ōtepoti,
recording my genealogy in my fluffy pink notebook,
heading toward my papakāinga to look for answers,
stopping at every tidal pool I see on the way to soak,
mix-n-match mermaid fantasy.

'There are no Māori mermaids,' another artist says
in my DMs, 'only marakihau. You're so colonised.'
Okay? So pick me up and swap my tail out for my skirt,
make me walk around and do the things that would
satisfy you. But you will never be satisfied with me.

'I want to touch,' they whine, stamping their feet,
'I want to dress you up, cut your hair,
wipe the makeup off your face and tear
the tā moko off your arms.'
Market me as a butterfly babe. A moth maiden.
Ballerina bookworm. Disco diva.
If it says 'Pounamu Princess' on the box
it will sell.

I don't want to be moved around anymore.
I don't want to be touched by you.

I want to
touch myself.

Until I hear the call to come,
come back to the places that
slipped between the cracks of
your life.
Bring your Barbies,
let's play.

Horse girls

We used to ride the school benches at lunchtime, gallop with invisible reins in our embroidered jeans, or tie pink Jelly Jump Rope round our waists, pulling each other across the field, daughters of *Saddle Club* and mossy hills, hello world, this is me, life should be, growing and growing and taller we go, into longer legs and thicker manes, velvety treasures lolloping from pub to flat to bed, fun for everyone, braying over Tinder, counting each lover, another tuft of dust kicked up by a golden hoof.

Our people are great riders, we know from the old days cos there weren't any reigns until 1840. I suppose I've grown into my reins, their oil shine and leather clasps, pearl buttons and metal locks, they excite and delight, a stimulus from the naval to the nape, something to push and pull against with the throat.

But imagine, to ride freely? To clasp a bristly back and, with no more than a nudge on the hip, fly beneath the pelvis of Ranginui? To merge with the bone of the horse and become a wisp of racing smoke? To bend weightless in-between realms once thought lost, to exist as a myth and shed all sides of the self? To bruise the inner thigh a gentle shade of plum and unfurl with a curl, from the shadow of the church, into transparent delight? To gallop into the sunset with stomach and breasts and teke and heart bouncing proudly, aware of our mortality and the explosions of pleasure and love?

That is what we ride for.

Siren song

We were once fish
now we are mermaids
and I wouldn't mind so much
if the metamorphosis had been easier,
if we'd met in the middle,
if they hadn't hoisted me out
of the ocean onto dry sand
and left me to whoop and heave
with the hook still in my neck.

Pania of the Reef
was my most checked-out
picture book at the school
library
Pania of the Reef
who was born in the sea
but betrayed by a man
what's new?

Cooked Christianity going in
and nuns whipping the reo
out of our mouths no wonder
I throw up so much
trying to rid my stomach of the
acidic lies they fed us while we slept.

A pearl skin sack with a hidden tail
always half in and half out.

'There are no Māori mermaids,
only marakihau. Fearsome. Vengeful.
Hungry.'

We used to be fish
but now we are marakihau
large, lumbering and dangerous
full of puoro and wero,
ready to drown our enemies.

The Māori portraits

I went to talk to you today, to whakanoa,
but you were in storage to make room for another exhibition
I really needed to talk to you I thought it could just be us
kanohi ki te kanohi I could communicate my conflict we
could trace our threads together you would remind me . . .
but I feel so alone grubby face stained with tears smelling
like the sweat of a toddler forced to hold it together scrambling
for the exit a colder wind cups my chin I am sitting
outside the Art Gallery curled against the stone wall
so this is why we write ekphrastic poetry!
Sometimes I struggle to see you through the
fog of ash past the security guarding
our taonga . . . from us . . . I have to conjure you in my
own words it was never to say how pretty you were
it was always to feel you close as home
and sit at these stone walls, less alone.

Tangi hotuhotu

In the bowels of the museum I first hear the story of Hine-Pū-Te-Hue. Years ago she opened herself up and inhaled all the rage and mamae of the atua who fought over the separation of their parents. She carried these storms in her round puku to digest, and then release as sweet music.

I walk between shelves of taiaha, mere, hīnaki and hue. They are dusty and jumbled, leaning across each other like fallen bricks. I attempt conversation with these elders but it's hard to hear what they are saying over the storm. I find photographs of our whānau in albums strewn across abandoned desks. I press them against my forehead and nose.

You're in a strange place, they whisper, as I breathe in. It's an in-between place made of metal, glass and miscellaneous time. The drawers that keep our cloaks rasp and wheeze as I pull them out and push them in, the feathers wiri and wave goodbye. Pounamu meditates within crates that creak, crouched in the corners. High up on the wall behind me I can feel the eyes of the pou pierce the back of my head.

Outside the museum, a face in the bush, pale face with green eyes. I hear a car coming, engine growling in the street. I confuse the sound with pūrerehua, the revving, the charging, the wood lashing through the air, scalding the lobes of my ears. I rush into the bush as the engine gets closer, whirling above my head.

The green eyes glow, they won't let me go, in the night it makes sense for me to plant myself amongst the shrubbery and launch my whole wairua like a slingshot into a tangi hotuhotu.

I am lodged into a space, two realms, like a cooking utensil between the oven and the fridge. I drink in what is sent to me and become a wailing watering can feeding the plants.

Is this healing or horror?

My boyfriend comes and picks me up,
slides me into the back seat of the car,
and I return to my flat completely empty,
so hollow that when the wind licks my eyes
they whistle.

Study notes 1

The more I learn about my whakapapa
the harder it gets.

> More knowledge leads to more questions,
> faceless names press themselves along

my body like the indents of a vanished bed in the carpet,
or the shadow of an ancient taonga

> taken from the wharenui,
> snatched before we could even have a hongi.

What birth rights we should have and know
by now have been flung

> further away by a swollen Southern drawl,
> playdough laws, venomous Catholic schools, shameful wero.

Our marae sit in what seems like another
dimension, and even if I could get there,

> I am not sure I would be welcome.
> I lie with my arms and legs snailed into

koru, protecting what little left there is.
The result of a history paper

> whose sections have been blanked out
> by musket men and high-school principals,

telling me I have to earn the answers
to myself.

A giant fish, a safe space, an ancient struggle

I once tried to pace myself
but the islands are vanishing
and cars are charging forward
trying to knock us over
so

I crack open my manawa
and feel for the fibres
I pull
until my blood line blossoms
all over my lap
and suddenly my arms are
aching and I'm hauling this
blood line to shore
it doesn't stop

Hī! Hī! Hī!
it is anchored in the seabed
where Papa sends her pain forward
and tremors snake up to strike my
hands, electrocute my arms
ngaukino has weathered
this rope
but it doesn't stop

it was braided long before
time was budding
so I pull
legs bent like Māui with his fish
the skin of the sea wrinkles
and twitches an
irritated giant asleep

it takes hours
I consider stopping
but whenever I pause the line
tenses and moves slipping back
into the deep
and I cannot lose what I
have found
but it's hard
I am small

and the mamae is almost
blinding I feel cramps
and spasms
blood in my throat
heart drumming in my ears
the sun bows his head
almost in embarrassment.

But I am trying.
I am using all my strength
why is it not coming?
The wind hears my cries and
presses light hands against my
shoulder blades
all it takes is a nudge and
I lose my footing

the line drops
I am flung forward and
hit the water's mouth
still holding on tight
I shoot deep into the gut
of Tangaroa

I am so afraid to drown
but this is not Te Kore
to my surprise

through the murk of man
past the manic moki and
decaying coral I see
my kin
waving to me
people of the sea
we always have been
and my blood line
takes me to them.

Slumber party

Clustered in a tight silk room between a glass coffee table and
a giant inflatable sea shell from Kmart, I never had so many takatāpui Māori in
my life before.

I'd been looking and looking since high school ended, after the era of shame when
I avoided the monthly Māori lunch and kapa haka, and hid from myself when

my first friends tried to measure my blood in beakers from the science room,
moaning about handouts and Māori whānau hating on Māori whānau.
We've hated ourselves for too long.

But now, us, young in flesh, old in wairua, picking at acrylic nails, exchanging
author names, 'you MUST read this – every Māori must read this!'
we practice nothing but aroha,

spilling red wine into the carpet, smothering it with milk and salt because I heard
somewhere that cleans it out, there is no friendship quite like this, there is no
kōrero

quite like takatāpui Māori kōrero, secure in a safe space which we fashioned for
each other, years in the making.

White roses, lavender, kawakawa leaves in hot water, broken heru and bone on
glass, pink fur coats and icy blue eyeshadow

Lana Del Rey playing on vinyl, black, brown, red and blonde hair woven out from
each other's sacred skulls, lips of the ancestors fluttering like the wings of
pīwakawaka, we have much to discuss

planning the revolution.

Utu

Slip into the water,
call the atua to practice,
you are a pulsing piece of
pounamu ready to be blessed,
you are the pakiaka of the tree
raised to trip the hiker,
a burst of foam
on the cheek of Hinemoana,
the space between the embrace
o tō kuia moko kauae
you are the huia feather in her hair.
You are proof of resilience,
a one in a trillion chance.
Your gentle voice
swells the bays
and the bush,
sending shivers down crooked
spines beneath blue collars
and ironed suits.
You have no idea
how afraid of your mana
they are,
you are the utu
they didn't see coming . . .

Spitting on the statue of Captain Cook

I've been saving up my spit since I was five years old.
That's why my mouth was so dry through all those debates
with schoolmates and teachers, best friends and boyfriends,
'Why can't you speak Māori then?'
'There's no full-blooded Māori left so what are you on about?'
'Better off being colonised weren't you . . .'
'You were gonna kill each other off anyway.'
'Where would you be without colonisation?'
I couldn't answer then because the saliva I needed
to lubricate my defence was waiting,
brewing in my puku.

I saw you for the first time on the cover of a
school text book about NEW ZEALAND
I did not connect your brooding, doughy face with
the reality that I could not recite my pepeha for years.
When we reached you at the harbour,
I saw my partner and his sister spit and I panicked
and walked back to the car because auē, my mouth was dry still,
at the sight of you I felt my lineage shake,
we know what you were, we don't need to read the information plaque,
and I felt, dare I say it, mamae for you.
You, so severed from the natural world that you felt you had to dominate it,
mamae for you and your people, bound like tired green tomatoes or dried-up
sunflowers to the sticks of monarchy, growing crooked and sour,
mamae for people desperate to prove themselves to a clueless queen,
mamae that I put everything onto you, one man, because I have to,
the figurehead for the beginning of our colonial trauma,
you are a cog in the wheel,
but I hate you anyway,
I hate you, I weep for you,
I hate you.

I walk back to you
despite my stress, and going against what tikanga I was raised by
(to not spit in public),
I release 381 years of fury, self-doubt and resentment,
in one thick, silvery wad.

Watch your step when you walk past because it's still there,
clinging to the stone.

The bay is still and the birds are not singing

We have to work every day
to stay safe from rāwakiwaki
knowing that we are not supposed to
be here.

Instead of walking to the marae
to share knowledge,
I walk to a desk so that
I can pay rent for a flat that I do
not whakapapa to.

Instead of using my hands to
harvest harakeke in accordance
with tikanga and my human body,
I use my hands to write
poetry in secret behind the
computer screen so the boss can't see.

We are supposed to be our own storytellers,
songmakers, earth painters, trauma breakers,
with roots so long and strong they grip
the fingers of Papatūānuku like newborn
baby hands, never letting go.

I take evening walks beside the train track
where the trees cover up the road
and I imagine that there are no roads
no cars and I am back . . . and then wonder,
when am I going forward?
Imagine being back . . .
Imagine going forward . . .

So please
when you are speaking to us
remember
that you are lucky you get to
speak to us
because we are not supposed
to be here.

Reading Ranginui Walker in rāhui

Ka Whawhai Tonu Matou,
it is a struggle without end.
Uncles locked in white stone,
jailed for protest, Ngāpuhi rebels,
influenza epidemics, and classroom hidings from
men of God who gave us muzzle-loaded
guns whilst preaching love and light.
Fine print replaced tā moko.
Fresh ink on our faces,
confused in translation.

Short-fuse shadows cradle guns around poorer neighbourhoods and
prisons are stuffed to the brim. Tangata whenua separated from the warm earth by
a floor of concrete, the body of Papatūānuku cast like she has a broken leg, and we
are so distracted by to-do lists and self-help books.

How To Survive The City You've Been Forced Into.
How To Eat and Pay Rent and Not Get Evicted.
How To Breathe Underwater Without Gills.
'Don't forget to Reuse Reduce Recycle,' we were told
in school assemblies, while the government reused
our koru, reduced our reo, and recycled our people
into a workforce that rubbed away at their wairua
like sandpaper on the tongue.

Is this a nightmare?
Will we be woken up one day by our children,
carrying us from the car to the house,
citing pre-colonial facts and writing
essays on tino rangatiratanga?
Is this a dream?
Our wairua wanders,
Our mauri remains.

Māori spy

I am a great actress,
I am a Māori spy,
watching from the office,
the wheels churning,
cutting paper money pretty paper money,
plugging throats with dollars . . .
though I don't earn much,
I collect information,
education, tips and tricks on
how to get by
in this factory built around me.
I'm an undercover agent for my
whakapapa
ticking boxes to
prove my existence.
Little do they know . . .
I'm slipping tikanga into their wai,
and the kaupapa into their kai.
Little do they know I'm
rising, rising, working
tirelessly at their game,
to change it.
Āke, ake, ake.

Ahi kā

was lit long ago
and delivered into your chest
straight from the womb.

Your atua protect your genitalia
and offer you advice on how to look after
your nails, your jaw bone, your cranium.

Eventually we all return to garden
in our backyards, on the tooth of Te Pō,
green gloves and grey hair, lips of rose and

licks of kūmara blossoming.
We were always meant to play
but we were shoved into governance

and told to hustle or die.

Kōmingo

If I opened my knees like the ground opens during an earthquake, would you return?

I used to brush my hair outside and let the strands drift into the trees until I read *The Makutu on Mrs Jones*. I had originally wanted birds to use my locks for their nests. I always liked the idea of parts of my body weaving themselves into a natural kete for pēpi to feel safe in.

That's what I hoped my poetry could be. But I have since learned this is no longer a good thing to do. The risk is too great and the hair could strangle small creatures in their own homes.

Perhaps my poetry is no good for us either. Perhaps my poetry could lull us into soft sunset sleep, then suck all the air out of us like a vacuum.

I brush my hair inside again, use it for my own nest. I invite another coloniser into this bed every second night. I whisper unedited spells into their ears as they fall asleep and by dawn my words have bruised their necks violet. This almost makes up for my not celebrating Matariki every year.

I thought we'd travel more, to cliffs that nudge the sky with wide nostrils and part them in a single exhale, surpass light pollution, shoot up to sit with a small fire and pūkeko on our shoulders.

The sisters would dance and our passed loved ones would come to sit with us, warm and grinning. I love to hear them joke and tease, we're a crack-up bunch. I listen to our intergenerational trauma enough, some nights must be for intergenerational joy.

I want to change my name back but I'm scared people will think I'm taking something beautiful from our nan without giving anything in return.

The Pākehā tongue is expensive and it cuts like the nail sticking out of the basement door that hooked into the palm of your hand when you were eight.

I am torn between the nurturer, the bridge, the lover, and the wrath, the eruption, the punisher. Imaginary criticisms stick like sunburn. Go bush for a while and they'll fade.

If I opened my knees like the ground opens during an earthquake, I doubt you would survive the fall.

There is a taniwha in my heart and a manaia on my head

I'm an Aquarius, and this means that no one
can ever seem to sum me up effectively
in readings or memes.

Aloof, standoffish, but usually well-liked,
on the website that I use to check my chart
my rebellious spirit is classified
as a weakness.

I never felt more tapu than when a Pākehā boy,
who just said he wished he was Māori so he could get tā moko,
and prided himself on performing haka in between his slam poems,
tried to slide his hand up my skirt in the back seat of my friend's car.

And I, freshly emerged from the lake,
took his head in my mouth and
bit tightly round the spindly neck.
Ate his mana up. How dare he.

Exited the passenger seat like Paris
exits her Ferrari. Head down, swiping my
sweet glossy blood-stained lips with a diamond nail,
bracelets giggling on my wrists.

When I say I am reclaiming my Māoritanga,
I am not saying it like I'm picking up a hobby,
like golf or stamp collecting.

I am saying it with the full force of a chest
slit wide open ready to be operated on,
with small lizards wandering up my thighs
as though time were against them,
I am saying it with my grandmother's spine
in my throat and the pūkana of Tūmatauenga
in my eyes.

Aquarius Aunty
is here for you.
Put your head on her lap,
tell me what he did,
I will gobble him up.
There will be blood.

Land Back.

Can you name the local iwi?

Land Back.

Do you talk to the local iwi?

Land Back.

Do you know pre-colonial stories?

Land Back.

Signs at tourist hot spots explain gold-mining history
but don't mention whakapapa Māori.

Land Back.

Can you look at the river without jumping in?

Land Back.

We will never be millionaires.
The world does not pay for truths.
The Crown does not uplift the indigenous.

Land Back.

How many secrets sleep beneath luxury villas?
Wealthy gentrifiers move on to Waiheke Island without protecting Pūtiki Bay.
Trademark Kia Ora and call it a day.
Skip a couple dozen steps to get to the goods,
good allies filling up all the classes, racing to fluency with aroha, but leaving the
rest of us back in the dust.

Land Back.

What version of Te Tiriti did you read?

Land Back.

If you read it at all?

Land Back.

Whose land do you walk on?

Land Back.

Who is the land you walk on?

Land Back.
Land Back.
Land Back.

Pretty pūngāwerewere

Scaling my maunga for the first time ever
trying not to misstep wandering wahine
wastrel woman hybrid hottie
pretty pūngāwerewere
crawling up the path fringed in snow
sheltered by kāmahi

Eight legs to twelve heavens sharp spinneret
on my behind webs like a choir
am I a katipō or a *Dysdera crocata*?
It's freezing here in August but
I am a pūngāwerewere in a pink korowai
on the hunt for a kai clouds of feather keep
me snug the tree bark here is orange the moss is
green and green goes so well with pink

I know I have grown from fallen berries
I was crafted from the groin of Hineahuone
I arrived on a ship from England
and a waka from Hawaiki
all in a coiling tide one before or after
the other rosehip pricks my legs bloody
whakapapa envelops me smothers me
I climb tirelessly to the soundtrack of
kaumātua weeping

Oi can you skip this one? I don't like it

Sell me a song in the reo that was
seized from my grandfather's lips
send me a postcard from Pātea of us doing
the haka advertise the creation story and paint
a tiki wearing a santa hat in the dairy window
Kiwiana makes me retch I can't believe
I used to think it meant Māoritanga ew
Māori myths and Māori maths are all up
for debate but why don't we deconstruct
and embrace the ingoa Pākehā so much?
Come so far to build on stolen land
after being colonised for centuries
short memories and selective hearing but
we need to talk about our role here

It may be a bit of a shock because I have
spun myself into a nest of my own
personalised echo chamber with other poets
and artists who prize kotahitanga and
manaakitanga over gumboots and pavlova
but I am happy to venture out
to catch you little flies and spin you in
your own excuses my spinning wheel
spinning web I excrete all the way up
the maunga catching the curses of our
predecessors in sticky silk sacks.

Goddess of death

My thighs are strong like kauri trunks
I could quite easily crush your beautiful neck
between them
as you try to climb inside searching for
immortality.
I like to tease you because I know you can
sense it is close
that portal of your own origin that centre of
endless
indiscriminate energy it is burning at my core
even though I cannot control what is within me
I know it is there.
When Māui died, all the taonga he stole or
was gifted
returned to the wāhine of the world and here
in us you will find them.
Our jaw bone hooks you in like an island and forms
passages for the mouth to mould around
enchanting kōrero and lilting love language,
the final surviving unbreakable rope laced with the hair of Hina
sprouted out from the skin of our scalps long ago,
and we wear it proudly in plaits, with heru and feathers,
in messy buns or pixie cuts,
and you know the children of Mahuika never died,
we fished them out of the water and clicked them
onto our own nails,
wore them until they dried,
bursting into flames once more,
a reminder to you –
beware our touch,
we are ancient at birth,
when we fuck our eyes glow
white and memory moves our
bodies in the unholy rhythms that
they wanted us to forget,
a promise dipped in caution,
if you continue to love me,
treat me right,
I might just grant you
the moon.

Dear Tūpuna 2

Shall I tell you my dream?

I have been sleeping, the crown of a bare island in the centre of a dusty duvet, curtained in fairy lights and spiderwebs. See me roll now. Feel the carpet wrinkle and sense the marama blanche. I wake my mother too, stir her clay skin, pull at her puzzling weeds with my whirlpool yawn. By some practical magical design, I emerge from the stained sheets to collapse fresh acrylic toe nails on the floor, one by one, cherry red, six inches, eight nails, eight toes, and my twisted, rolling body slides after. Kia tūpato, I mutter, I was only sleeping.

The skirts of grey buildings shiver in fear and hot mimi waters their lawns out front. Tents sprout up like clovers with cardboard signs. I wash my face in the salty tears of Te Moana-nui-a-Kiwa, I floss my fangs with stalks of pātītī, I tease the tangles from my hair with witch knuckles and pipi shells, and infuse leaves of karamū to consume and cleanse. I kiss Tūmatauenga on the cheek before I dress, squeeze my legs into thigh-high hot boots, beneath which I will crush man's jaw. A loose top of chain mail draped over large, swinging breasts, a skirt of iron piupiu to dance with the winds that filled the sails of our waka, and a heru made from the lost bones of my great-great-great-great-great-great-grandmother on my upoko. My eyelids, so large, swallow their beads of glowing green, which scan the hills sharply for those who disrupted the natural balance of the world, our mataora, our life cycle. Stretching, I trudge over to the wharekai. Breakfast is a gritty coffee and a plate of parāoa parai dripping in butter, cradled and expunged by my forked tongue. I am a bottomless pit. The sky father bellows laughter, ready for a show, prepared to throw bolts of lightning when shit goes down. Ākuanei koe i a au. Enough. There is mahi to be done. In this dream I am a protector sent to flood the channels built by dead men so that we can swim and fish again. Monster on the move. Crawling across Ngā Puke-māeroero. Belly dragging over ravaged farm land toward Waitangi. I am relentless, a searing comet soaring over trees and paddocks, an unstoppable warning. Kia tūpato. Ka haere mai ahau.

And then I wake. I am small and soft again. I am alone in my bed, sweating and silent. I am no fearful power. I'm conversing with tūpuna who are at odds with each other.

I analyse the family tree my sister made for me for my birthday. I see many names I had never seen before, many souls looking to disappear or find a home. Whispers in my ears, pūkana in my heart, knives at my fingertips. How nasty are some of you? I see me in you, wanting belonging, ready to fight. I see me, Pākehā and Māori, looking for my place on the whānau tree.

What do I need to do to get on with things? I am not frightening and I have no lessons to teach. Where do I put this rage? I'm listening.

With love,
your mokopuna.

Summertime surgery

Bathe

Unable to visit the womb of te moana, I tumble into the belly of the bathtub, unsteady,
shrunken to the size of a cat's eye, or a *Lunella smaragda*, chiselled from her pāua bed.
From shallow water poi āwhiowhio rises with the steam, shades the ceiling in a thick
mist, miraka, butter, miraka, in between my teeth and my toes. Whose knees are these?
Whose baby hairs and pocket of belly fat? I bleed with maramataka on my wrists, koiri
unwind from the centre of my spine, outward push. It has been quiet lately. The birds
are abundant and the weather is unusually warm, it is time to meet myself. In water
I may. In water I drape my heavy, rippling thighs across my knees, my abdomen presses
against my hips, my arms braid around my neck, my hair tangles into my hair, and
I whisper the exact same words from my lips to my ear to my lips to my ear.

Bed

Tacky threads grow out from my belly button, weigh me down like a silt curtain.
Sinking into silence, I finally feel the wormhole embrace binding my ankles to the
floor, my gut wakes me up in the early hours and I am reduced to a growling carnivore,
poisoned by what feels like years of scheming. I call a doctor and they want to cut me
open. I call my tūpuna and they guide me through the procedure. 'Grasp the wires with
two hands and pull, pull, pull. There is a matau lodged in your body, and it is time to see
what it caught.' A poem wriggles out from a celestial hole and falls onto my lap, stamps
poutama onto my skin, and my blood cleanses whatever paihana remained. The dam
is broken, I stare at this wet result that once swam inside of me and cry and laugh.
Mihimihi. I will be grateful till my eyes finally close.

Birth

I sit up, a 25-year-old child.
A fine, barely cooked egg whose skin has been pierced. My yolk threatens to cover the
whole plate. The clock on the wall pales and we are left with no pace, no measurement
of joy, no counting down of grief. Just ourselves just our bodies just our organs, just the
thunder and lightning inside our thorax and peeling lips pressed against each other,
and I am in love. I reach for the bent back beside me, kiss the nape, count the moles,
trace the pillow creases. We will not be here one day. Being plagues the thought process,
interrupts a good moe. Breathe. The first breath the last breath – our noses will never
separate – I participate in the giant hongi which swells across the motu –
A – ro – ha
A – ro – ha
Hā – hā – hā – hā
Listen to your protective instincts.
Listen to your origin story.

Wewete

I want to decolonise my body.
To brush the tangles of a history
loose from my hair
so that they disperse like
fish over a waterfall.

I want to decolonise my mouth.
Expand my reo beyond haere mai,
haere rā, pick the raru out
like tonsil stones from the
circumference of my throat.

I want to decolonise my wairua.
It is so slow and laden like
that stink spirit in *Spirited Away*,
I need more bath tokens.

I want to decolonise my eyes.
So that I see all the gifts of
our atua.

I want to decolonise my skin.
So that I may wear my moko,
feel the dew and sap and flax,
kawakawa and chamomile,
heather and horopito,
the muirs of Scotland merged
with the hills of the Hokianga.

I want to become the root raised
from the wet dirt, broken
through the concrete path,
to trip everyone up,
the exposed truth of a tree.

Ināianei

>   you are no longer
>   part

>   Māori
> or
>   %

>   you just are

Ināianei

>   you trust your whakapapa

> to know you as well as

>   or better than
> you know yourself

Ināianei

>   you enter Māori spaces warm

> as the kākahu that are your birth rights

>   hug your shoulders

Ināianei

>   you give relentlessly to your community

> despite your uncertainty

>   despite your doubt of belonging

Ināianei

>   whakatinana.

3. Manawanui

Orokohanga

Gardeners and voyagers,
people who soothed and fed,
led tamariki to the water's edge,
sung descendants into the soil.
I breathe for you,
I live for you,
I move with you.
My veins are whītau,
tendrils woven from the
hands of the first woken wahine,
they loop from the roots of my toes
to the ends of my hair,
labyrinthine, impossible to copy.
From Papatūānuku
we are born her taonga.

Study notes 2

The more I learn about my whakapapa
the easier it gets.

More knowledge leads to more questions,
pūrākau and ingoa indent themselves along

my body like footprints in soft grass,
or deep red markings of kōkōwai

foraged from an earth that keeps on giving,
despite all that goes against her.

What birth rights we should have and know
are being recalled and taught

in kōhanga reo, whare wānanga, and the ngahere,
kauae raro, karanga, maramataka, all coming home.

Our marae sit in reality and are tangible
once again, I can reach them,

I know I will be welcome because I am their moko.
I open my arms and legs to fan like the fronds of a

fern, embracing what is left.
Mauri tau. I am beyond the written page,

a gift back and forth, wound in tangling locks,
māwhaiwhai pūmahara, māwhaiwhai time,

there is no final here, only mō āke tonu

I whakapapa, therefore I am

Say I'm not Māori enough.
Say it to my face – the face of my tūpuna.
Look me in my Ngāruahine eyes,
tell me what I am again.
My cheekbones are Taranaki cheekbones,
I have healthy Hokianga hair.
Beware the wero of my Ngāpuhi tongue.
When you speak to me you speak to
my ancestors, my guides, my whenua.
My hands are as smooth as my awa,
my hips are as heavy as my maunga,
and my waka carries me still.
I know what I am,
I know who I am.
I am Māori enough.

Koro

My koro doesn't know I call him koro,
I think he'd just laugh and shrug if he did,
he doesn't know much reo anymore,
his mother tried to teach him, she was fluent,
but one wahine against an entire Catholic school
is a bit of an unfair fight.

My koro recalls his childhood at the kitchen bench,
I pry him with questions, finally old enough to listen.
He remembers his sisters dragging him to the beach
to collect pipi, kina, 'oooh crayfish was my favourite.'
It's too hard to get crayfish out here in the middle
of the country, it is hot and dry, the ocean is hours away.
He eats kūmara and potatoes, cabbage and tomatoes instead.
His garden is so tidy and he never sits down except to read
the local paper or drink a tea on a hot summer day.
It is always summer when we visit.

My koro tries to answer all my pātai, bewildered at my
interest. I am only just noticing his hair has thinned
more, his waist is smaller, his back has bent lower.
I record his kōrero on my phone.

My koro leans against the splintered fence and recalls
the time he ate kererū. I gape, jealous.
'It was everything you'd think it would be.'
Juicy, sweet, illegal. Just beautiful.
He tells me that his older sister used to work
at Whakarewarewa village in Rotorua but had to leave
because she was too impatient with the Pākehā visitors.

My koro misses our grandma, he only has sweet things
to say about her. He never remarried. He keeps her crystal
in the cupboard with the fancy cutlery.
He recalls life on the mountain, running a garage,
he tells us he wasn't allowed to play cards with
his army crew back in the day because he was too good.

They may have taken the words, but his reo is still inside,
I can see it speak out through his garden, his preparation
of dinner, his countless cups of tea, the way his creaky whare
has become our meeting house.

My koro waves from the driveway, crooked fingers,
gap-tooth smile, tidy shirts, our link in a long rope of
unbreakable muka rolled by his mother and her mother and
so on, our constant, our marker for home, we draw toward him like
moths to the ahi every once in a while, looking for peace in a
small place.

Eel dreams

In the middle of a cyan lake
I float above a carpet of writhing
eels.

Kaitiaki who cover the floor,
there is no rock or reed,
there is no shore in sight,

no place to stand,
when you have the mahi of
your whakapapa to pick up.

I swim,
the currents from their tails
pushing me forward,

there is no chance of sinking
when their jaws snip gently at
my nono.

Whānau mārama

Swinging my poi in the club I feel my
ancestors kick their heels and shake their hips,
my arms twirl high, high as the peak of Taranaki.
Shadow figures dance, dotted in starlight, I reach for them
with shells on my fingers and glitter on my arms,
bone liquifies, necks extend, folds writhe under lights,
a club full of kares who stretch all the way from Hawaiki –

dance with us
dance with us.

The night is young
and the land is the lung
the ocean the heart
and the moon is out and full.

The moon is the teat that we suck,
as well as the lover we fuck,
the moon is our mood ring, our waiata, our diary,
the moon is our cure, our tohunga, our hypnotist,
our salvation.

The moon is our mysterious, decadently dressed Aunty
who always gives us good books for our birthdays.
What do astronauts know of the daughters dowsing
themselves in waiwhero as though it were
spring water on a hot Hokianga night?

I'm swinging my poi in the club and I never felt
so hot before. I'm not alone right now, I have my
people –

dance with us
dance with us.

Put your head under

Strip the bands from the curls in your hair,
kick your legs free from the fabric and

put your head under

run your hands across your arms, your belly,
between the crests of your tapa o te kūhā,
just like your tūpuna did,
fingers like manu soaring,
cutting between mountain slopes
and river gorges,
feel the lashes and tresses of Hinemoana
mould around your figure,

put your head under

there are kaitiaki here,
the sand recalls quietly,
over and over,
and if you are very still,
you may hear
blessings, warnings, gossip,
eyes closed, salt up your nose,
you are at home in between,
used to squeezing your body
and mind,
part fish, part person,

put your head under

your hair grows an extra twelve inches
down here, your bones loosen,
your skin ripples, you can
release that sound,
pent up in the tomb
just below your ilium,
because the water
is listening
but the people cannot hear,
so will not ask what is wrong
when nothing is wrong or right,
everything floats,

you are a sea tangle,
rooted for a moment,
when you pass your fingers
gently
over the budding mussels clinging
to the rock,
their mouths may open to kiss you
home,

keep your head under

when you wash up onto the shore,
your tail dissolves, your skin dries,
you are the first being once again,
the first breath, the first sneeze,
exiting from your lungs,
you are orange like clay,
you are ready
to hold your head up
until the next
time you
put your head under.

Kōkōwai

I am a shapeshifter

    from rock to grain

powder to paint

        bold as the face of Hineahuone

            or rare blue like the pāua

who clutch the thighs of Hinemoana

        mix with oil or honey and

            lick me onto the brow

                stroke me onto a page

                    lover of lava

the pounamu round your neck

        kisses the mortar and pestle

            which moans and wails

    this must be what the stomach

        of an atua sounds like when they

are hungry

your brown hair catches

wet lines and flicks them

through whatever picture you

were trying to create because

the body cannot resist

playing with me.

I am everything that made you

I am the genesis of your tinana

from my many blankets

in the ground you have grown

into flesh and bone

and for this reason, I will get

all over your skin.

I've missed you my moko.

Late night marae

This is a paradox,
this comfortable discomfort.
The deep snores rip and strip
slits into the space-time continuum
of which I fall through.
Trapped in a ribbed room with quiet
kōwhaiwhai and rumbling bodies,
rain tuts and spits outside,
time ignores us all.
I will not sleep tonight.
Open my eyes slowly,
peek at te poutūārongo,
crawl off the mattress to go
make a cup of something,
and absorb psychic noises on
the front porch . . .
Whai swim in circles on the
surface of my instant coffee,
the city hums over a hump of bush,
taonga puoro is hidden beneath
blankets of glass chattering,
but I hear a note
amidst the flax rustling like
pages of an old pukapuka,
there is the call, the karanga,
now and then at 3am,
the full moon karanga,
splitting the soul into pieces.
I open my ears wide
for the voice which chants:
                    be receptive to your tūpuna
                    be receptive to your tūpuna

Dear Tūpuna 3

I'm back to where I need to be.

My sister and I crouch in the front yard with a dead kawau pū manu between our legs, plucking the grey and black feathers from squishy flesh. We are practising making earrings and decorating our kete with the gifts from Tāne and Tangaroa. We trade what we've learned on the road and in our tutorials, this knowledge seeps into the grass at our feet like the juices of this manu. The garden will be especially fruitful this year.

It took me a while to find my feet. I had to go all the way back to where our waka landed to learn that I never actually had to physically go there to get closer to you. 'Chill out, kōtiro,' you whisper through my sleep, 'let go. It's not your job to hold up the sky.' I can't believe I actually thought for a second that you didn't have all the time in the world for me.

The self-doubt won't ever leave. There will always be someone at the back of the room spitting about what we look like, how we act. There will always be someone telling us we are asking for too much. Be grateful, catch up, times have changed.

I was fed so many empty words that lived in my puku like kutu, gnawing away at my internal lining, making space for more empty words. Now that I've stopped listening, there are these gaps and bite marks, desperate to be filled with rongoā.

So I drink kawakawa tea every few months and make balms with the recipe taught to me at the wānanga. I escort my colonial self back up the way we came, carefully unbuttoning the pearls on our blouses, shimmying the petticoats to our ankles, stripping the scales from our stockings. I turn over and glide my scissors down the back of our slimy corsets, then I check and scrub the corners of our naked wairua with warm water and kūmarahou. It's not about being clean, it's about being open. I let the ones with my best interests at heart in. You are with me all the way. My tail comes and goes.

I wake to feel you watching me, more and more of you, following me to the kitchen to pour hot water, to ready the coffee, standing at my side while I butter the toast, peering over my shoulder as I try to edit my poems. You choose the colours I draw with, guiding my pen along the page, out from you come these visions of moon maidens, eels, and mermaids.

These moments here and there I find in the middle of the day, this breath I am so lucky to have, my harrowing ribs rattling inside of me, they become still and secure when I think of you. This skin was made by you – the veins, the muscle, the branches of bones. I owe everything to you and yet, you ask for so little in return.

I will keep writing. Short letters now and then, asking impossible questions. I wonder what you would write back.

'Girl,' I hear it clearly now, 'you have nothing to prove. But that doesn't mean you don't pick up the tea towel.'

'Never stop giving,' you tell me, 'that's how you get. If you've got a little more, give some. You've got extra legs, hand back a few, you only need two. Activate giving what you were blessed with to your cousins, because then everyone can eat. Activate listening from beneath your high horse instead of on top of it. Activate community conversation and save your sweet tears for bedtime. Dig your way into the core of the kōrero you hear, before taking some blind offence. Strive to be the wise pūngāwerewere we know you can be.'

So in between tasks, doing the dishes, brushing my hair, before starting a new book, tumbling through te reo classes, strapping on butterfly heels, drawing naked ladies, in the back of my mind I ask these pātai . . . What can I give today? What are my tūpuna trying to say?

When someone I love comes to me crying, I tell them to write.

Write to your tūpuna, and they will reply through you.

I am forever listening.

With love,
your mokopuna.

Raranga

Softening harakeke on the front porch,
running a butter knife along ribbon strips,
smooth smells, blistered thumbs,
shuffle of blades slipping into and out of
place, muka rolling over the knee,
clumsy patterns and wonky endings.
The moana rolls and froths on the horizon,
the awa slinks and bends with its eels at my side,
Tāwhirimātea frolics through my loose hair.
I work, remembering three, five, ten
years ago, and letting go of my old aches,
seeing myself as a part of things that grow,
handing over my future to my tūpuna
who speak from the earth,
speak as the awhi rito,
he mutunga kore tō tātou aroha mōu,
our love for you knows no bounds,
I expect nothing
but for you to live
in aroha
in atawhai.

Kupu Māori

Note: these translations are very basic. Te reo Māori is an intricate language, and many words do not have direct translations into English, but require interpretation and a broad perspective.

ahi kā	burning fires of occupation
āke, ake, ake	forever/evermore/on and on
ākuanei koe i a au	I'll get you! I'll deal to you! You'd better be careful
āria	tidal pool/deep water between two shoals
aroha	love/affection/caring
atawhai	kindness/generosity
atua	ancestor with continuing influence/gods/deity
auē	howl/groan/wail
awa	river/stream/creek/canal
awhi rito	the mature leaves that protect the rito (younger leaves) of harakeke
hā	breath/essence/taste/breathing
haere mai	welcome
haere rā	goodbye
he mutunga kore tō tātou aroha mōu	our love for you knows no bounds
heru	sacred comb to adorn the head
hongi	to press noses in greeting
hotu	to sob
ināianei	now/at present
ingoa	name
ka haere mai ahau	I am coming
kākahu	clothes/garment/uniform

kai	food
kaitiaki	custodian/guardian/caregiver
kanohi ki te kanohi	face to face
karamū	small trees with pale bark and large leathery glossy leaves
karanga	formal call/ceremonial call
karukaru	blood
kauae raro	lower jaw/terrestrial knowledge/earthly knowledge
kaupapa	topic/policy/matter for discussion/issue
kawakawa	pepper tree
kēhua	ghost/spirits that linger on earth after death and haunt the living
kete	basket/kit
kia tūpato	be careful
kōhanga reo	Māori immersion kindergarten
kōkōwai	red ochre
kōmingo	to swirl/eddy
kōrero	speech/talk
koro	elderly man/grandfather
koru	spiral motif
kuia	elderly woman/grandmother
kupu	word/vocabulary/saying/talk/message
kutu	lice/parasites/vermin
mahi	work/job
mamae	be painful/sore/hurt
mana	prestige/authority/power/influence/spiritual power
manaia	sea guardian/carving

manawanui	to be steadfast/stout-hearted
manu	bird
marae	courtyard/the open area in front of the wharenui
marakihau	sea creature/guardian
maramataka	Māori lunar calendar
matakite	prophetic/visionary/person who can see
mataora	life cycle
Matariki	new year
matau	fish hook
maunga	mountain
mauri	life principle/life force/vital essence
mauri tau	to be calm/peaceful in spirit/relaxed
māwhaiwhai	spider web
mihi/mihimihi	to greet/pay tribute/thank
mimi	piss
miraka	milk
mō āke tonu	forever/forever and a day
moe	sleep
mokopuna	grandchild/descendant
muka	prepared flax fibre
Ngā Puke-māeroero	Southern Alps
ngahere	bush/forest
ngaukino	trauma/distress/pain
nono	bum
ora	life/health/vitality

orokohanga	origin/beginning/creation
paihana	poison/toxin
pakiaka	root of a tree
papakāinga	original home
Papatūānuku	earth/earth mother
parāoa parai	fry bread
pātai	question/to ask
pātītī	grass
pepeha	your story/link to your ancestors/form of introduction to establish identity/place
piupiu	waist-to-knees garment made of flax
pīwakawaka	fantail
poi āwhiowhio	whistling gourd
pōtangotango	to be intense darkness/pitch-black/pitch-dark
pou	post/upright/support/column
poutama	stepped pattern of tukutuku panels and woven mats
pūkana	to stare wildly/dilate the eyes
pukapuka	book/letters/lungs
puku	stomach
pūmahara	memories/sagacity
pūngāwerewere	spider
pūrākau	myth/legend/story
rāhui	reserved/restricted access
Rarohenga	underworld/where the dead go
raru	conflict/trouble
rāwakiwaki	intense grief/depression/despair

reo	language/dialect/tongue
rongoā	medicine/treatment/remedy
tā moko	traditional tattooing
taiawa	channel/passage/vagina
takatāpui	queer/gay
tamariki	children
tangi	to cry/mourn/weep
tangata whenua	people of the land/indigenous/people born of the whenua
taniwha	spirit/water spirit/powerful creature/monster
taonga	treasure/of value
taonga puoro	singing treasure
tapu	be sacred/prohibited/restricted
tāwara	murmur/buzz, hum (of conversation)
teke	vagina
Te Kore	realm of potential being/The Void
te poutūārongo	back wall post of a meeting house
Te Moana-nui-a-Kiwa	Pacific Ocean
tapa o te kūhā	groin/crotch
tikanga	correct/procedure/custom
tinana	body
tino rangatiratanga	sovereignty/autonomy/self-government
tohu	sign/mark/symbol
tohunga	expert/priest/healer
tūpuna	ancestors
upoko	head

utu	repay/revenge/compensation
wahine	woman
wāhine	women
waiata	to sing/song
wairua	spirit/soul
waiwhero	menstruation/menstrual flow
wānanga	seminar/conference/meeting
wero	challenge/stabbing
wewete	to untie/unravel/analyse
whai	stingray
whakamā	to be ashamed/shy/bashful/embarrassed
whakanoa	to lift tapu
whakapapa	genealogy/lineage
whakatinana	embody/manifest
whānau	family
whānau mārama	celestial bodies
wharenui	meeting house or large house
whare wānanga	traditional sites of higher learning/university
whenua	land/placenta
whītau	flax fibre

He Mihi

This pukapuka could not exist without the guidance and aroha of so much and so many.

First and foremost, I mihi to the whenua that I walk, dream and write on, to Kāi Tahu whenua, as well as my own whenua in Taranaki and the Hokianga. To my maunga, for watching over me, and my awa, for keeping me cleansed. To my tūpuna for being with me always and giving me everything that I have. To my iwi, Ngāruahine, Ngāti Ruanui and Ngāpuhi, for calling me home, and to the atua, for all of your gifts and guidance.

Thank you to my mother, Anna Carr, for always surrounding baby me with art and books, and for being such a selfless role model.

To my sister, Rebecca Carr Neave, for being my best friend and always calling me in when I need it.

To my nieces and nephews, for simply existing and being beautiful.

To Grandad Pehimana Koroneho Benjamin Carr, for being our home since forever. You mean everything to us.

To all our aunties and uncles and brothers and sisters-in-law, and to the Pakaua and Inwood whānau, for all your aroha.

Arohanui to Miriam Jenkins and Renée Sadlier, my sisters, for always being there; even when we're far away from each other, you are the two I turn to knowing I'll never be turned away.

To all our friends who I cannot list because it would be too long and I'd feel sad to leave any name out, you know who you are: thank you for all the games nights, *LOTR* nights, Paris nights, dirty Dunedin nights, for all the coffees and tears, deep wānanga and dumb jokes. I love you.

To my darling Matariki Pakaua Inwood, thank you for always being there for me, with me. You know there are no words so: bum.

Thank you to Emma Neale for being my teacher. Your devotion and immediate willingness to look over my work meant so much to me. You gave me such constructive feedback and pushed these poems to get to where they needed to be.

To Tayi Tibble, for inspiring me as a poet and also for being one of the first sets of eyes on this text. Your notes were so solid and perceptive, I appreciated them greatly.

I would like to acknowledge the amazing Anne Kennedy and Kiri Piahana-Wong, for both being so patient and helpful. Your insight and edits have shaped this pukapuka to be so much sharper and stronger.

A huge thank you to Georgia Gifford for helping me with my reo in the opening, and Te Aniwaniwa Paterson for reading through my final edits. Thank you to Trinity Thompson-Browne for all your edits and wānanga, and to Emma Terina Smith for also guiding me through my reo.

To Nadine Pehi for all your hard mahi with our whakapapa, and for sharing your knowledge so generously.

Huge mihi to my literary inspirations: Witi Ihimaera, Keri Hulme, Ranginui Walker, Patricia Grace and Jane Austen (to name a few).

Warmest thanks to Sam Elworthy, for giving me this dream-making opportunity and being so patient with my editing process.

And finally, thank you to my creative community, both offline and online, for seeing me as an artist, for engaging with my mahi, and supporting me in every sense of the word. You've lifted me up, you've inspired me to try new things, and you've taught me so much.

This pukapuka is for you.

Jessica Hinerangi Thompson Carr is of Ngāti Ruanui, Ngāruahine, Ngāpuhi and Pākehā descent. Born in Ōtepoti, she has a degree in English and art history with a masters in Māori ekphrastic poetry. She is a poet, journalist and illustrator, working primarily on Instagram under the name @maori_mermaid. Her previous work has appeared in *Landfall, Starling, The Big Idea* and *The Pantograph Punch*.